D1136569

How to Lead a Seeker Bible Discussion

Rebecca Manley Pippert

InterVarsity Press
Downers Grove, Illinois
Leicester, England

To Ruth Siemens,

My mentor, my friend and
a true hero of the faith,
whose life has shaped not only mine
but countless others around the world.

I dedicate this series to you—
with gratitude beyond expression.

InterVarsity Press
P.O. Box 1400, Downers Grove, IL 60515-1426
World Wide Web: www.ivpress.com
E-mail: mail@ivpress.com

Inter-Varsity Press, England
38 De Montfort Street, Leicester LE1 7GP, England
World Wide Web: www.ivpbooks.com
E-mail: ivp@uccf.org.uk

©2003 by Rebecca Manley Pippert

InterVarsity Press® is the book-publishing division of InterVarsity Christian Fellowship/USA®, a student movement active on campus at hundreds of universities, colleges and schools of nursing in the United States of America, and a member movement of the International Fellowship of Evangelical Students. For information about local and regional activities, write Public Relations Dept., InterVarsity Christian Fellowship/USA, 6400 Schroeder Rd., P.O. Box 7895, Madison, WI 53707-7895, or visit the IVCF website at <www.ivcf.org>.

Inter-Varsity Press, England, is the book-publishing division of the Universities and Colleges Christian Fellowship (formerly the Inter-Varsity Fellowship), a student movement linking Christian Unions in universities and colleges throughout the United Kingdom and the Republic of Ireland, and a member movement of the International Fellowship of Evangelical Students. For information about local and national activities write to UCCF, 38 De Montfort Street, Leicester LE1 7GP.

Cover design: Cindy Kiple

Cover and interior image: Stewart Cohen/Getty Images

U.S. ISBN 0-8308-2121-X

U.K. ISBN 0-85111-789-9

Printed in the United States of America ∞

P	15	14	13	12	11	10	9	8	7	6	5	4	3	2	1
Y	13	12	11	10	09	08	07	06	05	04	03				

CONTENTS

WHAT IS A SEEKER
BIBLE DISCUSSION?

One October afternoon I was in my car on the way
to my friend Nancy's home where we were about to
start a seeker Bible discussion for our neighbors in Naperville. As I pulled into Nancy's drive wondering
which of my neighbors would actually come, I found
myself thinking back to how I first became interested
in seeker Bible discussions.

College Days

It was the summer after my junior year abroad at the
University of Barcelona. I attended a Christian international student conference at a castle called Schloss Mittersill, nestled in the Austrian Alps. With students and
speakers coming from all over the world, it was like a
mini United Nations gathering for Christians. Little did
I imagine how that month would change my life and
shape my ministry for years to come. Over the next fifteen years I returned seven times to Schloss Mittersill.

I heard extraordinary teaching from many different speakers, but it was two women, Ruth Siemens and Ada Lum, who had the most profound effect on my life.

Ruth and Ada led a seminar on evangelism in which they asked the question, "How do we arouse our non-Christian friends' interest in the gospel?" Most people are not ready to receive Christ after hearing the gospel only once, nor are they usually ready to come with us to church. So what do we do? Ruth and Ada's idea was compelling: Invite seekers to read about Jesus through studying one of the Gospels. Many people who are resistant to the idea of attending church are still curious about the Bible—especially if they have never read it. Regardless of whether the seeker discussion format was one-on-one, a small group or a larger group, Ruth and Ada had found it to be one of the most effective ways of sharing Christ.

"But will nonbelievers really come?" someone asked.

"Yes," they responded, "because many seekers don't find it as threatening to meet with other seekers to study the Bible as to attend a meeting where the majority of the participants are Christians."

"But most seekers don't accept the Bible as God's Word or believe it is true!" one student spoke up.

"But we aren't asking them to!" replied Ada and Ruth. "Simply point out to the participant that the Bible is the primary source document of the Christian faith. We aren't asking them to believe it—just to see what it says."

It made sense: if people want to understand Marxism, for example, they need to read the *Red Book*. They don't have to be Marxists in order to read its primary source material; likewise for anyone investigating Christianity. The issue is to be informed enough to make an intelligent decision.

"Tell them they should think of the study more like a book club," Ruth and Ada said. Then they added, "Of course *we* know this is far more than a book club. The Bible has the 'ring of truth.' God's Word will not only inform seekers, it will convict, give life and transform!"

I loved the idea from the moment I heard it—having a Bible study in which the majority of the participants were *not* Christians intrigued me. But I had serious reservations. First, I was a young believer, and I had never led a Bible study for Christians, much less non-Christians. What if I was asked a question I couldn't answer? Furthermore, as a young Christian I had almost no Bible knowledge, so how could someone as biblically uninformed as me lead a Bible study? And would seekers really be interested? I had lots of non-Christian friends, but I couldn't imagine they would be interested in reading the Bible.

Yet I was so inspired by the teaching of these remarkable women and amazed by their absolute confidence that seeker Bible discussions really "worked," that I made a commitment then and there that, with God's help, I would start my own seeker Bible discussion in my second semester of study at the University of Barcelona. I prayed and asked God to lead me to open seekers, and eventually I invited five students to a seeker

Bible discussion. They not only came, but they in turn asked other seekers to come. (The full story is told in the first chapter of my book *Out of the Saltshaker.*)

Without exaggeration I can say that the Barcelona Bible discussion changed my life forever. I saw with my own eyes that non-Christians are truly interested in reading the Bible if approached in the right way. I learned that I didn't have to be a Bible scholar to lead a Bible discussion; I just had to be prepared and let the text speak for itself. I discovered firsthand that the Bible has its own power and authority to speak to minds and hearts. I saw the Spirit of God open blind eyes, convicting and wooing seekers to Christ. I saw a divine power at work that went far beyond my feeble efforts. Best of all, I saw several of my friends become Christians.

From that point on I was a "convert"! No one ever again needed to convince me that seeker Bible discussions are a powerful tool for evangelism. Since that time, I have led seeker studies for professionals during their lunch breaks; neighborhood studies for suburban housewives and couples; and studies for teens, college students and the elderly. I've seen seeker Bible discussions used for men's groups, faculty, golf pros, inmates in prison, church planting—you name it. I have led seeker discussions with only one other person and with three, eight, twelve and twenty people.

The First Gathering

There I was on a lovely day in October, about to walk into Nancy's home to lead a seeker discussion for my neighborhood. This seeker study was the culmination of prayer, plans and preparation. Nancy and I had made a list of the people we wanted to invite and began praying for them daily. Since we knew that to be a true seeker discussion the majority of people had to be seekers, we invited only four Christians to start with and gave them this stipulation: in order to come they had to bring one seeker friend. Besides making our own personal invitations, we also held a coffee gathering for a larger group of neighbors during which we invited anyone who wanted to come to our seeker Bible discussion.

As I walk into Nancy's home, I am greeted by the smell of coffee brewing and the sight of food arranged on the kitchen countertops. The chairs in the family room are arranged in a semicircle, the room is well lit, the dog has been tucked away, and Nancy's phone will soon be turned off. Everything about the home says, "You are welcome!" When the guests arrive, we are thrilled to discover that nine seekers have come; counting the believers, that makes a group of fifteen.

The composition of our group is varied, with Unitarian, Protestant, Catholic and Orthodox traditions represented, as well as the unchurched. There is a dramatic range in beliefs: some are agnostics; others believe in God but aren't sure what they think about Jesus; some think being a Christian is the same as being a Girl Scout or an American. Their only common denominator is a fragmented understanding of Christianity and the fact that few of them have read the Bible as adults.

We laugh in relaxed conversation and catch up on

each other's lives while drinking coffee and munching on the simply prepared food. After about twenty-five minutes I suggest we go into the family room.

The First Discussion

We have purchased Bibles, and as the Bibles are being passed out to those who need them, I again state the purpose of our study: "This is for people who are interested in discovering who Jesus is and what the Bible has to say. It's for people in various places on their spiritual journey. This isn't a study for people who've got it all figured out—it's a safe place to come with honest questions." I mention some basic discussion guidelines, I share general information about the New Testament (found in chapter three, "Leading the Bible Discussion: Practical Discussion Guidelines"), and I talk briefly about John, the author of the book we are reading. (This information can be found in my John seeker studies.) My introduction takes about ten minutes.

Now I ask the introductory question. I like to use the first question each week to break the ice and arouse the curiosity of the seekers. Since we are about to read John 2, I ask the very first question printed in my study guide: "What are common complaints people have against religious institutions such as the church?"

Initially there is a surprised look on their faces like, *I know the answer, but isn't it rude to say it in front of the Bible?* Soon someone pipes up, "Well, some people say the church is full of hypocrites."

"Exactly!" I answer and the others nod their heads

in agreement. "Anything else?" I ask.

"Well, my husband always complains that the church is just a money-making machine," says another woman. Now there is laughter and more nodding heads.

Then I say, "Well, guess what? It was no different in Jesus' day. We are about to read a story in which Jesus takes on these very issues: hypocrisy and religious leaders making a buck off people in the name of religion. You may be surprised to see how Jesus responds."

That's all it took—the seekers are hooked. Because the question touched on such a common criticism the world has about the church, they are now eager to see how Jesus responds. Since this is our first meeting, I am not surprised that it takes time to really get the conversation off and running. I express enthusiasm over their contributions and delight when they offer a slant on the passage that I've never thought of before. Seekers have a way of seeing the humanity of the text that believers often miss.

After about fifty minutes I say it's almost time to wrap up. Then I ask the final application question found in each of my study guides called "Live what you learn." In the John 2 study the question is simply, "What would you say to a person who complains that all Christians are hypocrites based on what you have learned about Jesus thus far?"

After several minutes of conversation, I close, but I tell them if they stick around I'll try to answer any questions they may have. Then I tell them what passage we'll be reading next week, and I pass out the study guides for those who don't have them already. I explain that if they want to read the passage ahead of time, or even answer the questions in the study guide, that's great. But I strongly emphasize that there is *no homework*. We don't want people not to come if they haven't read the passage.

Many stick around, and the feedback is very encouraging. They express surprise that the Bible isn't as hard to understand as they thought it would be; in fact, they now think it's stimulating and fun. A few even ask if they can bring a friend next week. I drive home full of gratitude and joy.

When we started this seeker Bible discussion, we assumed it would meet for eight weeks, but we have now been meeting for two-and-a-half years. After the first year the group became too large for me to lead alone, so I chose seven mature Christian women from the group to lead separate seeker discussions the following year. As I write this, we are now in our third year, with three separate Bible discussions that meet in Nancy's home at the same time but in various parts of the house. Many seekers have become Christians and are attending church. They are now bringing *their* seeker friends to the study, and one woman who came is being trained to be a coleader for next fall.

I am as convinced by the power of seeker Bible discussions today as I was as a college student in Barcelona. Besides demonstrating the love of God to seekers, there is nothing more important than drawing them to consider Jesus. People simply don't know who Jesus is or what he is really like. When seekers are willing to look beyond their stereotypes and take a fresh look at Jesus, the scales in front of their eyes begin to fall. I've never seen a person yet who hasn't been fascinated to encounter the Jesus of the Gospels.

Even we who know him need to be renewed. I am convinced that one reason for the freshness of my love for Jesus is that I keep rediscovering him as I read the Gospels with seekers. I listen to their observations; I hear their amazement as Jesus shatters their previous stereotypes; I am refreshed by their original insights on Scripture.

Why Are Seeker Discussions So Effective?

The idea of an evangelistic Bible study is not a new method of evangelism. But it is a neglected one. When Philip went to the Ethiopian in Acts 8:26-40, he asked questions, listened carefully and, beginning with Scripture, proclaimed the good news of Jesus. In this case Philip was doing a "one-on-one" seeker discussion, which is often a good place to start.

A seeker Bible discussion is a group discussion (be it two people or twenty) around a passage of Scripture, usually starting with one of the Gospels, that vitally confronts the participants with the person of Jesus Christ. It is aimed for people who have a confused, vague or fragmented knowledge of the gospel. The purpose of a seeker discussion is not to present a complete case for biblical Christianity each time. The ultimate goal is for seekers to submit their lives to Christ as Savior and Lord. But the immediate objective is to have any personal, positive encounter with the real Jesus.

Seeker discussions are different from regular Bible studies that are geared for Christians. The questions in a regular Bible study assume faith and ask practical application questions that apply to believers. In a Bible study for non-Christians, the questions do not assume the person answering is a believer.

Seeker discussions communicate truth in narrative form. In the past, many Christians thought that as long as we presented the facts of the gospel in a logical order people would respond. But as Ruth Siemens writes, "In spite of the rejection of absolute truth, many in our pluralistic, post-modern culture have become skeptical of the *scientific truth* approach of modernism."[1] Today's seeker is usually less interested in a lecture based on the facts of Christianity than in a narrative approach that reveals truth through story form. But won't non-Christians today, long entertained and overstimulated by movies, TV and the Internet, find a Bible study a bit dull? Not if we invite them to consider the story, to "get inside the skin" of the people we read about in the Gospels; to watch Jesus as he relates to people, listen to what he says and discover what he thinks. This kind of approach has enormous appeal to today's seeker.

In our desire to direct people's attention toward Jesus, we need to remember how God captured the at-

---

[1] The quotes from Ruth Siemens are taken from an unpublished paper titled "Investigative Bible Discussions."

tention of the people in Jesus' day. He used terms that human beings could understand. That is what the incarnation is all about—God became one of us, and we cannot neatly divide the human nature of Christ from his divine nature. We must first grasp the facts about Jesus' humanity before we can approach the majesty of his deity. This was how the disciples came to understand Jesus, and so will it be for our seeker friends.

Seeker discussions are process-oriented. Seeker discussions appeal to moderns because they honor process. Today's skeptics are not comfortable with a fast, rushed, sign-on-the-dotted-line kind of approach. They need time to absorb and process what they are hearing, and by using a seeker discussion approach, they can learn the core truths of the gospel without feeling pressured. Since many non-Christians have no religious background and no familiarity with the Scriptures, they don't have much understanding of a Christian worldview. It's not simply that they doubt whether we are made in God's image and yet are sinners—they aren't even sure what those terms mean. Therefore, they'll need more time to absorb and learn what the Christian faith is about. By meeting on a weekly basis for six to eight weeks, seekers can gradually learn the core truths of the gospel without feeling rushed or manipulated.

Seeker discussions are dialogical. Seekers today want to dialogue as peers in their quest for truth. They want an open forum in which they can ask questions and wrestle with issues. They resist an approach that is top-down, where we do all the talking and they do all the listening. However, the Bible discussion leaders should not feel intimidated by the fact that seekers come with questions. What I hear most when I train others in how to lead seeker Bible discussion is, "I'm afraid to lead a seeker study because they'll ask questions I can't answer."

As discussion leaders, we need to remember two things. First, establish up front that we are going to focus on the passage we are studying rather than get off on a tangent such as, "What do you think about reincarnation?" Second, to seekers, dialogue is much more important than debate. I rarely find seekers today who come wanting to trump me with a question. That used to be the case, but times have changed. Whether or not we can answer their questions seems to be far less important than whether they sense we are *hearing* them—taking seriously their questions and respecting where they are on their spiritual journey.

Seeker discussions promote authentic relationships. Seekers today need to know that we love them and are authentically relating to them; otherwise they won't trust us. The apostle Paul said of his three-week preaching mission that laid the foundation for the Thessalonian church, "We were delighted to share with you not only the gospel of God but our lives as well, because you had become so dear to us" (1 Thessalonians 2:8). We cannot share the gospel of Christ unless we are ready to share ourselves as persons—authentically relating to them as persons, not as objects of our evangelistic efforts. That's one of the reasons why meeting in a home is helpful—because it offers a personal touch. (However, I do know of several successful seeker studies that are meeting in a church.) Seeker Bible discussion is a patient, realistic, friendship-type evangelism backed up by personal concern for people's needs. In the discussions, seekers will begin to see the difference Jesus makes in the lives of the people in the text, but they will also begin to see the difference Christ makes in our own lives beyond the text.

Seeker discussions promote understanding of Christian community. I have always been fascinated by how seekers seem to pick up, almost as if through os-mosis, what Christian fellowship is about. Even though we don't pray out loud or sing hymns or pass a collection plate, seekers still seem to grasp something about Christian community. Just the fact that they are reading the Bible and discussing the topic of God with other people is quite a significant experience for most people. One woman in our Naperville study said to me, "I have known my neighbors for years. We play tennis and go to our kids' soccer games and band concerts. But I never thought I would know my neighbors on this level." Then she said in a whisper, "I still can't get over that I am actually talking with my neighbors about—you know—*God*."

Prayer is a significant part of Christian community. As Christians we take it for granted that when a need is voiced, we offer to pray. But what we consider com-monplace is often a deeply moving gesture for a seeker. When someone shares a personal need with me privately after the study and I respond by saying I will pray, I am sometimes told, "Oh, do you think you should bother God with this when he has so many important matters to deal with?" What a wonderful opportunity to share how God is concerned with every detail of our lives! There usually comes a point, especially after trust has been built, in which someone shares a need and asks the group if they will pray. That is often the first time they have ever asked others to pray for them. As a result of requests like this, I've seen astonishing answers to prayers prayed by people who haven't even committed their lives to Christ! God is alive, and he wants them to know that he is there, that he hears their prayers and that he loves them.

There is a woman in my seeker discussion whom I will call "Sally." She had never read the Bible or been to church. One day she walked in, and I could tell by her face that she was shattered. Afterward I asked her what was wrong. "My husband has just been diagnosed with cancer, and they have to operate immediately. Oh Becky, if only I had a strong faith like yours, but all I do is cry." She told me the date of surgery and said, "Would you please ask the group to pray?" I told her I would. That night she called the hostess of our study, Nancy, and asked her for the Scripture Nancy had referred to that day—a Scripture Nancy said had strengthened her in a difficult time. Nancy told her the psalm and assured her of her prayers.

Because our group is made up of seekers, I was uncertain of what their understanding of prayer might be, but at the next study I shared Sally's prayer request. Several weeks later Sally returned absolutely beaming. Speaking to the group before we began, she said, "First, I want to thank you for praying. Before I came to this study, my husband and I had never discussed the subject of God, and we'd never read the Bible. But the night before his surgery, I read him the psalm that Nancy shared with me, and I told him you were all praying. Reading that psalm, talking together about God and knowing people were praying for us—that's a real first for us.

"The next day I felt such peace," Sally said, "During the surgery the doctors kept reassuring me that everything was going beautifully. But suddenly a doctor came in and said my husband had begun to bleed profusely, and they were worried. I ran out of the waiting room and headed straight for the chapel. But when I got there, the door was locked and a sign said 'under construction.' This was the only time in my life I had ever visited a chapel, and it was locked! I was so distressed that I didn't know what to do.

"Suddenly a nurse took my arm and asked me what was wrong. When I told her, she said, 'I'm the head nurse on this floor, but I've just gone off duty—would you like me to pray with you?' I nodded my head yes.

"She told me she was a born-again Christian, and I told her, 'Well I'm in a Bible study for seekers, but I've never prayed with another person before; in fact, I've hardly prayed at all.'

"She nodded her head in understanding and took

my hands in hers, and she prayed the most powerful prayer I've ever heard. Then she walked me back to the waiting area just as the surgeon walked in saying, 'Wonderful news! The bleeding stopped just a few minutes ago!'

"So I must tell you two things: First, I now know that God is real. I'm still trying to figure out most of this faith stuff, but I know he cares about us in a personal way. I mean, what's the likelihood that the head nurse would spot me, be a Christian and refuse to leave work without praying with me? And my husband told me that as far as he knew, no one had ever prayed for him before. The night before surgery he was scared to death, but early that morning, before anyone had come in, he suddenly felt a peace he'd never experienced before. He believes it was God answering your prayers, and he wants me to thank you with all his heart."

Of course there was not a dry eye in that room. Interestingly, it took another two years before this precious woman accepted Christ as her Savior. But God in his mercy and grace had revealed his power and love to all of us in an unmistakable way.

Seeker discussions are spiritually powerful. Most of all, seeker Bible discussions are effective because we are tapping into God's richest resources: the power of the Word and the power of the Holy Spirit! Over the years I have seen how the Holy Spirit speaks through God's Word and makes it come alive to seekers. Most seekers are amazed to discover that they really can understand the Bible. As one person in my seeker discussion said to me recently, "I never read the Bible because I assumed it would be impossible to understand. I never dreamed the stories would touch me so, that Christ would seem so real and that the Bible would be relevant to my life."

We may deceive ourselves and hide from the truth, but once we engage the Scriptures and the power of the Spirit begins to illuminate its truth, we find we can't hide from ourselves or from God. So, when we are doing a seeker discussion, we must remember that we are using powerful resources from God. On our own we can not reveal Jesus. It's the power of his Word and the Holy Spirit that mysteriously and supernaturally reveals Jesus, erases blindness and awakens faith.

Seeker discussions are advantageous for believers. For most of us, seeker discussions are a much better use of our time and resources. Through a seeker discussion, we are able to connect personally, share God's Word and demonstrate the reality of faith in Christ. Think of how much more truth we are able to communicate in a six- or eight-week study than we ever could in one sporadic conversation.

We also learn effective personal evangelism as we listen to seekers each week. What seekers think usually differs from what Christians expect! How often do we have the opportunity to ask seekers questions and then listen to their answers for several weeks running? When we have a seeker discussion, we don't have to worry about how to bring up the subject of God. A weekly study enables us to discuss different aspects of faith without our needing to broach the topic. And if we should meet one of the seekers for lunch, we know so much better what they are thinking, where they are struggling in their faith and what they don't understand. And our friendships become stronger as we meet weekly.

Seeker discussions do not require us to be professionals! Nor do we have to have the gift of evangelism to lead a seeker discussion. Not every Christian can preach a sermon, but nearly everyone can learn to lead discussions—even a new convert like me, when I lived in Barcelona. Furthermore, seeker Bible discussions build up our faith as we begin to see people change and some even become Christians.

CREATING A SEEKER-FRIENDLY ENVIRONMENT

The main ingredient for a seeker-friendly environment is the love of Christ. Jesus continually stressed and demonstrated the necessity of a life that bears the profound stamp of God's love. Jesus received people as they were. He didn't insist that the woman at Simon's banquet demonstrate her gratitude for having her sins forgiven by asking her to exegete Ezekiel. He allowed her to touch him, to weep over his feet and dry them with her hair. Why did Jesus respond to people in this way? Because Jesus said he was revealing his Father's essence.

How do we create an atmosphere that reveals Christ's love? I asked Diann, a Bible study leader who has a special gift for making people feel welcome and loved, what makes for a seeker-friendly environment.

Diann's Tips

In a seeker-friendly environment, no matter what is

said or asked by a seeker, there ought to be an atmosphere of acceptance and warmth that communicates that this is a safe place to ask questions, seek answers and find out who God is. We created a friendly environment by starting our meetings with a social coffee time. We also made phone contacts and planned one-on-one meetings between group sessions. I could see that the more the group members felt acceptance and trust, the stronger the foundation was for studying Scripture together.

I think my friend Mary's story provides a good example of how a welcoming environment can reach a seeker. Mary, invited to a seeker discussion by a neighbor she didn't want to offend, only intended to attend one session. Mary was in her early sixties and she was a genuine intellectual— extremely well read and very curious. She had never read the Bible, but she jumped right in and began asking lots of questions. She liked the way we approached Scripture—how we challenged people to think, without demanding faith. Yet it was clear she felt torn. Her fascination and intellectual curiosity kept her coming back week after week, but there were times she would physically bristle when she didn't like what she was hearing. I often felt very intimidated by having such a penetrating mind in my group, and I continually asked the Lord to help me. Since she was such an intellectual, I assumed that if she ever became a Christian, it would be by way of her intellect.

I was bowled over when she told me one day, "You know, all my life I've felt like I was on the outside looking in. I felt like there was some kind of club that everyone else had been invited to except me. But in this group, I have found acceptance and love, and people I would have assumed had it all together have admitted they have problems and questions just like me. I think this is the first time in my life I have ever sensed people cared for me just as I am. And it's made me less judgmental and critical of myself and others. More than that, God has started to become real to me, not only because of what I am reading in the Bible but through the love of the people in our group."

In the two years that Mary has been in my study, she has changed dramatically. In the beginning she was skeptical, with sharp edges, but as she felt accepted, affirmed and nurtured, her demeanor softened and she became more open to the Scriptures and to other people. This year she came to the realization that she needed to do more than just intellectualize what she was hearing. She realized that faith required a personal commitment to accept what Christ was offering to her. No one in our Bible study will forget the day that Mary dropped the bombshell: "When I first came to this study, I thought of myself as a real heretic, but by the end of last year I had moved from a heretic to a skeptic. But this year it finally all made sense, and I felt compelled to do something about it. I have given my life to Christ." Recently Mary wrote a note in which she said, "God has worked overtime through this study to get this reluctant one to accept His grace, but here I am, a believer in Christ at last."

The 8 L's

I have developed a list of principles, which I call the "8 L's," that will help you create a seeker-friendly atmosphere. The overarching principle is the love of Christ, and what follows is simply the practical working out of his love.

Love. Show genuine appreciation, interest and delight in each person attending (1 Corinthians 13:8; 1 John 4:7-21). One way Christ's love is communicated is through the small group experience itself. Seekers learn about the Christian faith not only by what is taught from the Bible but by what is "caught" as seekers see our love, our honesty about our own trials and our desire to pray for them in their struggles.

Listen. One form of expressing respect and love is to carefully listen to what they say. What questions are they asking? What problems do they have with faith in general or with the particular passage being studied? Try to put yourself in their shoes.

Laughter. Show seekers that Christians know how to have fun! We need to relax, lighten up and be spontaneous. Create a relaxed, casual, "unchurchy" atmosphere. If there is anything that kills seeker Bible discussions, it's judgment from Christians. Laughter helps bring people together, rather than dividing them.

Language. Avoid using Christian clichés and unnecessary theological terminology. Always try to express religious ideas in plain English so seekers don't feel you are speaking a different language. For example, if I use the word *salvation* because it's in the text, then I might add, "That means to become whole, to be united to and reconciled with God so we can become the person we were meant to be."

Learn. Your authenticity is established as they see you as a fellow learner. We don't come with all the answers, with nothing to learn but everything to give. Seekers will give us new insights into the text because they are seeing it with fresh eyes. When they say something from a fresh perspective, tell them, "That's a wonderful insight. I'd never thought of it that way before!"

Lift them up. The secret to having a Christ-filled, loving atmosphere is to invite Jesus to be present. Pray for each seeker to be comfortable, to experience the presence of Jesus, even if they can't articulate why they feel drawn to us or to the study. It is important to ask other Christians outside of the study to diligently pray for your study and for the seekers. They will be blessed to hear of their spiritual progress. If, by chance, there are some Christians who are nervous about your friendship with non-Christians, enlisting them to pray may cause them to become supportive of you rather than critical of you.

Low key. Be unshockable! If someone makes an off-the-wall comment or says something doctrinally wrong, you might say, "That's an interesting idea. What do the rest of you think?" Be careful not to be doctrinaire or dogmatic. Ruth Siemens was leading a seeker discussion once when a very drunk woman came barging in, disrupting the entire study. Ruth quickly summarized the rest of the passage and served refreshments. But Ruth's kindness and graciousness toward this woman turned out to be the catalyst for one of the seekers giving his life to Christ!

Lunch. Sometime during the Bible discussion series take at least one of the members out to lunch. Or plan one social event for the whole group apart from the study—perhaps a Christmas brunch in the coleader's home, as Diann did.

LEADING THE
BIBLE DISCUSSION

A seeker discussion almost always begins by studying Gospel passages to watch Jesus in action and learn who he really is. Jesus gave his disciples time to observe him in all kinds of circumstances. He didn't clobber them over the head and say, "Don't you guys get it yet that I am God?" When John and Andrew first asked him who he was, Jesus said, "Come and see" (John 1:39, 46). As they accompanied Jesus and observed his *humanity*, his *deity* eventually stood out in sharp contrast.

They soon believed that Jesus was Messiah, but it took longer to be convinced that this Messiah was God. Jesus gives them time, until near the end of his ministry when he asks, "Who do you say that I am?" Then Peter courageously says aloud, "You are the Christ, the Son of the living God!" (Matthew 16:16 ESV).

As a Bible discussion leader, your goal is to lead people to this same discovery by making the narratives come alive for them. Ask the kinds of questions that let the seekers interact vicariously with Jesus through the characters in the story. That way they are really interacting directly with Jesus, because he is as present in your discussion group as if he were sitting on one of the chairs—as present as he was in the story you are reading.

Be careful not to explain away Jesus' humanity. Do not say that because he was God, Jesus risked nothing when he touched the leper. Or that he always knew people's thoughts. The Gospels make it clear that only sometimes did he use his prophetic insight and power. Jesus became one of us and accepted our limitations, yet without sin. As you read Gospel passages with seekers, you will see Jesus thirsty, hungry, sleepy, tired, feeling the pain of betrayal and in need of prayer. The mystery is that it is out of his humanity that we begin to see his deity.

So put yourself inside the skins of the people. Ask yourself, *What were they feeling? What would they see, smell, hear?* As a leader, aim for a "you-are-there" kind of flavor. Lead the discussions in such a way that you feel the suspense and emotions of the original encounters.

Using a Guide

Many Bible study guides are available—but not many are specifically evangelistic. Be careful that you use material that has been written for seekers. The best approach to use for seeker Bible discussions is inductive—where you examine the details and let them lead you to the conclusions the text demands. (A deductive method begins with conclusions and seeks proofs.) An inductive study guide consists of questions and notes to assist leaders in helping participants discover inductively and quickly what it took someone else much longer to dig out. The questions in a good inductive study first ask us to

1. *observe* what the passage says.

2. *interpret* or discover what it meant for the writer and the first recipients in their culture, and correlate that data.

3. *apply,* or determine how it applies, to us today.

Remember, a seeker discussion is not a theological study, nor a lecture on apologetics, nor the sharing of experiences. It is primarily a question-guided discussion. The leader does not give a talk or sermon, because our peers usually won't accept us as religious authorities anyway. A leader helps participants to examine the text for themselves so that God may speak directly to them through the pages of his Word.

One comment I frequently hear when I train people in leading seeker Bible discussions is "But I don't feel I am an authority on the Bible. Wouldn't I have to study for years in order to lead a study?" My answer is that *we* are not the source of authority—the Bible is! The role of a good inductive Bible discussion leader is to be a "guide on the side" not a "sage on the stage"! Here's how to do it by following the four P's.

1. Proper Preparation

I asked Anne, an excellent Bible study leader and one of the leaders of our Naperville seeker discussions, what she felt was important to being a good leader.

"Proper preparation was really key for me. Even though I've led Bible studies for years, sometimes I still have doubts and anxieties. I especially felt an added responsibility since these women were seekers. So going into the discussions knowing I was prepared gave me the extra edge of confidence I needed.

"I prepared by becoming very familiar with the passage, reading and meditating on it daily. I prayed for insight into the text as I prayed for the women in the study. After jotting down my own questions and thoughts, I then started working through the questions and then, if necessary, I used a commentary. Last year we studied Luke, and, as with any prepared study guide, I found myself rephrasing, adding or deleting study guide questions. I'd often even write my own introductions if I didn't want to use the ones in the study guide, and I usually summarized the last lesson before we began.

"What encouraged me was to see the tremendous response of these women to God's Word. I loved their insights, honesty and fresh perspectives. As I prepared I would often think of the words in 2 Timothy 2:15: 'Do your best to present yourself to God as one approved, a workman who does not need to be ashamed and who correctly handles the word of truth.' "

Here are some basic principles to help you as you prepare the passage:

- First, find a quiet place to prepare, and as you read the text through several times, ask God to reveal his truth to you.

- Read at least two translations in your preparation.

- Write down questions or notes you want to bring up in the discussion.

- Answer the study guide questions—but feel free to add your own questions or delete questions that you don't want to use. Use the questions flexibly rather than mechanically.

- Use a commentary if you wish, but only after you have studied the passage yourself. (Commentaries can be helpful if you come across a phrase that is hard to understand.)

- Remember, study guides are not written in stone, so be flexible. I have never used a Bible study guide that I haven't had to tweak in some fashion—including my own!

2. The Power of the Word

Never forget you are dealing with dynamite when you lead a Bible discussion. Hebrews 4:12 says, "The word of God is living and active. Sharper than any double-edged sword, it . . . judges the thoughts and attitudes of the heart."

One of the chief ways that God speaks is through his Word. When people tell me they can't lead a Bible discussion because they feel inadequate, my response is, "Don't worry about whether you have self-confidence—it's *God-confidence* that you need!" The primary source of God-confidence is God's Word; the Bible has the "ring of truth." The Hebrew word for *truth* means "reality"—that which actually is, the world the way

God made it. Nonbelievers cannot live by their world-views because they keep bumping up against the Creator's reality. Over and over again I have seen seekers surprised by how powerfully the Bible speaks to them. God means it when he says that his Word "shall not return to me empty, but it shall accomplish that which I purpose and shall succeed in the thing for which I send it" (Isaiah 55:11 NEB). So ask God to make the passage you are studying each week come alive to you first and then to the seekers in your discussion group.

Several years ago I led a seeker discussion for very successful professional women. One woman I invited was an influential executive who agreed to attend mainly because of our friendship, but also because she felt that any intelligent person should at least be familiar with the Bible. Her attitude was mildly disdainful and aloof. She clearly felt she was doing the Bible a favor by reading it. But a few weeks into our study she said, "Through my job I meet some of the most powerful people in this city. In fact, I can spot a powerful person a mile away. But I have to tell you—Jesus is without question the most powerful person I have ever encountered."

The next week she continued, "What fascinates me about Jesus isn't just the fact that he is so powerful—it's how he *uses* his power that intrigues me. He uses it to love and serve others, yet there's never any question that he's in charge." Another week she said, "I know this is going to sound weird, but all week I kept thinking, *I wonder what Jesus would think about how I use my power at work?*" And the following week she admitted,

"You're all going to think I've lost my mind, but last week I found myself wanting to ask Jesus if he thought I was living my life the way I should. But then I'd stop myself and say, *You don't even know if you believe in Jesus, so why does his opinion matter so much?*"

How can you possibly explain her response apart from the power of God's Word and Spirit? My friend came assuming she would judge and assess Jesus. But after a few weeks of reading the Gospels and encountering Christ, she felt as if *she* was the one being assessed, and she even wanted his input! Her story confirms Hebrews 4:12: "The word of God is living and active."

3. The Power of the Holy Spirit

Another source of our God-confidence is the Holy Spirit. " '[It is] not by might nor by power, but by my Spirit,' says the Lord Almighty" (Zechariah 4:6). Only the Spirit of God can reveal Jesus and make him come alive to seekers as they read his Word. We also need the Spirit to give our own words meaning and life. It is so easy to forget Jesus' words that "apart from me you can do nothing" (John 15:5). In the final analysis it is not *our* ministry but the ministry of God working through us. We must pray for the Spirit's power to work though us and to speak to our group. We prepare diligently and responsibly, but we are utterly dependent on God to speak to the hearts of unbelievers, to open blind eyes, and to use us in our weakness and limited knowledge. It is the Spirit of

God that changes lives, not human performance!

Prayer is one way to tap into the Spirit's power. One of the most important decisions the leaders of our Naperville seeker group made was to meet a full hour before the study to pray. We would go over any questions we had in the text, but we devoted most of our time to prayer. We prayed, by name, for the people coming to the discussion. We asked God to open their eyes, to bless them and their families, to help them see Jesus and to create a desire in them to give their lives to him. It made all the difference. Prayer is an absolutely essential part of any seeker discussion plan.

4. Practical Discussion Guidelines

From the start, encourage open discussion. The group discussion is a critical aspect of the study because the participants are not passive listeners. Group members need to be fully absorbed in analyzing the text and sharing their findings. The leader's role is to guide them with questions. As Ruth Siemens writes, "A truth that *participants* discover in the text makes more impact on them than a truth we present."

You need not begin a seeker group with prayer. Your guests have come to find out what the Bible says and to learn about Jesus, but they have come thinking this is more like a book club. The apostle Paul did not pray at the Areopagus! If you prefer to pray, make sure it is simple and not long-winded. For example, you might say, "When I study God's book I like to ask for his help." Then pray briefly.

Be mindful of timing. A good discussion leader makes sure to begin and end on time, even if he or she has to summarize part of it to get through the text. So it's best to say in the first meeting, "Let's try to get through the text in the next sixty minutes so we can end on time. But after the study is over feel free to stick around and we can talk about whatever you like." Plan to reach the midpoint before half your time is up, so there will be enough time to summarize the story and discuss the applications at the end. But be sure to finish at the set time.

In the first meeting, review the purpose of the study. Tell people, "We are here to see what the Bible really says and means about who Jesus is. The Bible, not the group leader, will be our teacher. This is for anyone with an open mind. This study doesn't assume you already believe in Jesus or that you accept the Bible as true. Rather, it's to help you make up your own mind once you know what the Bible actually says. We want this to be a safe place for anyone with honest questions. This is a discussion, not a lecture, so everyone is encouraged to participate."

In the first meeting, review basic facts about the Bible. Why do they call what we are studying the New Testament? (The Old Testament was before Christ; the New Testament is after Christ.) What does the word *gospel* mean? (Good news.) Explain that the New Testament begins with four books about Jesus' life written by four different men, most of whom were actual eyewitnesses to the events they write about. Share a few facts about the author of the Gospel you will be studying. Have them turn to the table of contents to see how to find books, and help them locate the book you are studying. Explain how all the books are written in chapters and verses. If you use the same translation then just say, "Please turn to page . . ."

Begin the particular week's discussion. For those of you using my study guide, now is the time to ask the "Discussion Question." The purpose of this first question isn't to share the main lesson of the passage—that would spoil their discovery of the text! Rather, it's to break the ice and arouse their curiosity in the text. After a brief conversation, read aloud the "Historical Context" before reading the passage. This will give them a context to better understand what they are about to read.

Read the biblical text. If the passage is short, it can be read all at once. If the passage is longer, read it one section at a time, asking the appropriate questions pertaining to each section. I don't ever call on a person to read. Rather, I ask if there is anyone who would like to read. If no one responds, then either the leader or the coleader may read it.

Use discussion questions to engage the seekers with the text. Leaders ask the main questions, using supplementary ones if necessary to help the group dig more deeply. Lesley, one of the Naperville Bible study leaders, taught me the importance of always writing extra questions next to the study guide questions in case no one answers or seems to understand the initial questions. She said having extra questions always gives her a sense of confidence as she goes into the study. Don't be worried about silent moments—give people time to think. However, if you ask the same question twice and they don't seem to get it, then ask your supplementary question. If they answer the question by reading the verse, ask them to restate it in their own words. Mere reading of the text can be dull, and you must gauge how well they seem to understand.

Don't correct all wrong answers immediately. Never say an answer is wrong. Because seekers usually don't know much about the Bible, they fear looking foolish. It's better to say, "That's interesting. What do the rest of you think?" Receive several right and wrong answers without comment. Then ask the group if any verse in the text clarifies the point. It is not humiliating when several people are wrong.

When participants ask questions, refer some of them back to the group. The leader does not "throw the ball" to each person in turn and receive it back. Anyone may catch the ball and throw it to anyone else. Let group members interact. When the ball drops, summarize and throw out a new question.

Keep the discussion on the passage as much as possible. If an extraneous subject comes up, jot it down for a private conversation. If everyone is interested, suggest a future study of that subject, using a more relevant passage. You might say, "That's really an important question you're raising. But since it doesn't relate to this text, would it be all right if we discussed it later?"

Be careful not to confuse seekers with too much

cross-referencing. Avoid unnecessary references to other parts of the Bible since seekers will have trouble finding the verses. However, ruling out all cross-references impoverishes the study. The leader should use relevant references from the immediate context in order to resolve "problems" in the text or enrich a lesson. It's good to show how we let the Bible interpret itself—just don't overwhelm the seekers with too many passages. Be deliberate.

If you can provide copies of the same translation for everyone, then do. Ask your local Christian bookstore if they can offer a readable translation at a discount. However, you could also say at the first meeting, "If you are going to buy a new Bible for this study, then I would suggest X version because that is the one I will be using, and it might make things clearer for you. But if you have a different translation from mine, then by all means bring it." Then explain how some translations focus more on readability, putting things into everyday English. Other translations try to be faithful to the original literary structure, but sometimes the language itself is a little harder to understand. The Bible I have most frequently used in a group is the RSV or the NIV. I definitely prefer a translation rather than a paraphrase for a Bible study.

DEVELOPING A
LEADERSHIP TEAM

If you anticipate having five or more in your seeker Bible discussion, I would encourage you to find a coleader and someone to host the study if you are the Bible discussion leader. I know of successful seeker discussions in which the same person leads and hosts the study, but whenever possible it is best to develop a small team of support, for your mutual encouragement and for prayer.

The coleader's role in a larger seeker discussion is important. Besides offering the leader support and studying the text with great care, the coleader is available to lead the study if the leader can't be there. Margie is an example of a tremendous coleader and a great support to Julia, who leads one of the seeker discussions in Naperville. Here's what she says.

Margie's Tips for Coleading

"I think the verse that best describes the dynamic relationship between a leader and a coleader is 'two are better than one, because they have a good return for their work; if one falls down, his friend can help him up' (Ecclesiastes 4:9). If there seems to be a stumbling block in the discussion, or if the conversation lags, or there's a point that needs clarification, the coleader can jump in and pick up the slack. I have thoroughly enjoyed my role as coleader. What I have found so spiritually stimulating is that Julia and I are a team—we both share the same vision and passion to see these women come to Christ.

"Most weeks Julia and I meet together. We bounce thoughts off one another and find additional Scripture to support or clarify an answer. We take time to pray for the women in our group, asking God to work through us and to reveal himself to all of us. If we can't meet, then we talk by telephone. I keep an updated roster of the women in our group so we can pray specifically and intelligently.

"Because the Bible discussion leader must pay attention to the biblical text, I take the role of watching for any nuances or body language. Then I can give Julia feedback on what I observed of the people during the study. If I sense someone is struggling, I'll call that woman during the week. Or if I see that someone is very shy or timid, I'll draw her out after the study. There was one woman in our group who was an avid reader and really digging for truth and solid answers. So I asked her out to lunch and gave her the book *The Case for Christ* by Lee Strobel. She gobbled it up.

"Being the coleader, I feel like I get to do the 'fun stuff.' Last Christmas our group met for lunch at my house, and at the end of last year's study, we went out to a restaurant. For these women, just having a chance to withdraw from a hectic schedule and be pampered and shown love was a revolutionary experience. At the Christmas luncheon, I gave each woman a heart with her name on it to remind her that the best gift she could give Jesus was her heart. At the end of our study in April we went to a restaurant, and I gave each woman a devotional to use for the summer. I knew the devotional was a totally new idea for them, but I thought it was worth a try—and it was a good way to keep them reading the Bible while we were apart. They loved it! A week later I received a call from one of the women, who said, 'One night I read the selection to my entire family and it seemed to have been written just for us.'"

Not every seeker discussion needs a coleader, but a team approach to seeker studies provides so much support and encouragement.

Hosting a Seeker Bible Discussion

If your group is larger than five, I would suggest that the host be someone other than the Bible discussion leader. The leader has enough to do to prepare for the study. Perhaps the coleader might host the study in his or her home. But if the discussion group is quite large, like our Naperville group, perhaps neither leader should be the host. We have a remarkable hostess in our seeker discussion. I asked Nancy if she had any tips for a person hosting a discussion, and she said, "We live in a society where bigger seems better. What a comfort to know that what people really need when they enter our home is the knowledge they are loved, welcome and a delight to have in our home. Trust me—people can sense it. So instead of worrying about whether everything external is perfect, focus on showing them God's love; have a listening spirit and an open heart—those are the really key ingredients to being a true host."

So what are some of the duties of a host?

- Be there early to greet people and make them feel welcome.

- Provide name tags.

- Make sure chairs are spaced properly and there's enough light and ventilation.

- Be sure to have extra Bibles on hand.

- Have beverages and simple food available.

- Take the phone off the hook once the study starts, or have someone assigned to answer it.

- Be sure animals have been put away during the study.

- Greet people with warmth and interest, and know their names.

BETTER
COMMUNICATION

One of the challenges of being a Bible study leader is learning to deal with group dynamics and the difficult situations that commonly arise in group study. Lesley is a gifted Bible study leader and part of the team that helps me when I do seeker Bible study training conferences. One of her areas of expertise is dealing with tricky people. Here are some of the areas she stresses.

Dealing with Tricky People

Talkative. A talkative person answers every question without letting others speak. You could say, "What do the rest of you think? Does anyone else have any other comments or ideas?" If it's repetitive behavior, you may need to enlist their help outside the study and ask them to help you to draw out the quieter ones.

Silence. Don't worry about silence while people are looking at the text for answers. Resist the temptation to answer your own questions. Give them time. However, if someone is persistently quiet, you could say, "Amy, what do you think?" or "John, what do you observe about Jesus in verse 2?" This is also a good place for the coleader to jump in if you have one.

Tangents. The Bible discussion leader asks a question about the birth of Jesus and someone asks, "What do you think about the Pope's view on birth control?" or "How could a loving God allow suffering?" You might respond with, "That's an excellent question, but could we save it until after the study?" Then be sure to discuss it with the person after the study. In the case of tangents it is helpful to remind the group of the purpose of the discussion: "Since we have so little time to actually study the text in front of us, let's focus on the issues the text raises and then deal with the issue you are raising at a later date, okay?" However, try to listen carefully to the Spirit. If it's an issue that really matters to everyone, sometimes it will be necessary to deal with it on the spot. But if you don't know the answer to the issue they are raising or if, like most of us, you don't think quickly on your feet, then say, "That is something I'd really like to think about. Could we discuss it after the study next week?"

Wrong answer. If someone offers an answer that is off the wall, you can rephrase the question, ask another question or say, "That's interesting. What do others of you think?" Sometimes you could say, "That is interesting. Now where do you find it in the text?" But avoid saying, "That's the wrong answer."

Sometimes, however, you are put into a position where you must tell them the answer is wrong. If that is the case then try to use some humor. I remember a woman once saying in a seeker study, "All of us become angels when we die, isn't that right, Becky? Doesn't the Bible teach that?"

I answered with a smile, "Actually that's more along the lines of De Capra and Hollywood than the Bible. I think you are thinking of Clarence getting his wings in the movie *It's a Wonderful Life*. It's a *great* movie—just lousy theology!" She laughed and that was that.

Dealing with Tricky Questions

Sooner or later in a study someone is bound to raise a difficult question; it is simply inevitable. So what do you do? First, remember to pray a quick, silent prayer for wisdom. God has promised to help us in all situations. Also, if you are unsure, do not be afraid to say, "I don't know." I have never found any seeker who is offended by that answer. In fact, they usually respect you more for your candid honesty.

Anne, one of the Bible discussion leaders in our seeker group, shared an incident that occurred right after September 11. Amy, a woman in her study, said that due to recent events she was now afraid to fly. That prompted Sue, another woman in the study, to say, "I carry a rosary in my purse because it helps me to not be afraid. You should try it." To which Amy responded by asking Anne, "Is the practice of the rosary in the Bible?"

Anne answered, "The practice of the rosary is a long-appreciated tradition in the Catholic Church. Though it's not mentioned in the Bible it raises an important point—how can prayer help us when we are afraid?" Anne was able to get the attention off of their differences and affirm what unites us—our need to pray.

Anne later told me, "I have learned in a seeker discussion that our purpose is not to set everyone theologically straight according to what we think is acceptable from our own tradition; rather, it is to plant seeds, to draw their attention to Jesus and to look for answers that the Bible offers."

I can't emphasize this point enough. As a leader we must show respect for different religious traditions. Our goal isn't to turn seekers into Baptists and Lutherans. Rather, our goal is to help them encounter the Jesus of Scripture in a personal, life-transforming way.

Anne recounts another story of the time when someone in her group said, "Can you believe that some people actually think there is only one way to heaven, and it's through Jesus?"

When several in the group seemed to agree with her, Anne felt she needed to address this issue directly. These seekers said they had no difficulty with someone accepting Christ—so long as that person didn't believe Jesus was the only way to God. Anne prayed a quick prayer for guidance and said, "That is exactly why we are here—to be able to ask the difficult questions and see what the Bible says. I agree with you that this is a very difficult issue to understand. It does sound strange to our modern ears to claim that anything is true in any absolute sense. We have been raised to believe that all truth is relative. Yet I have to be honest that Christ does claim to be the way of salvation. And if we accept him for who he says he is, as I have, then we need to accept his claims to be the Savior of the world as well. That doesn't mean it's always easy or that we understand everything fully, but I am willing to trust him at his word."

Anne said the women didn't seem offended; if anything, they were intrigued by what she said. But all that week she agonized and worried: *Should I have let it go? Did I say too much?* She was fearful that no one would return, and she prayed fervently. However, the next week there were more people than ever in her group, and several commented on what a good lesson the previous week had been!

What are principles for dealing with tricky questions? Wherever possible, agree with the person by finding any mutual common ground. For example, you might say, "I agree with you that this is really an important question and one that many have struggled with. And though it's beyond the scope of our study to answer this adequately, let me say . . ."

Here are several ways to proceed:

- In a winsome way state the biblical position and that this is what you believe, though you recognize that others may not.

- If you are asked a question and you don't know the answer, say so! "That's a great question, and I really don't know the answer. Does anyone want to investigate this, and we can take it up after next week's study?"

• If the question is valid but not relevant to the text, ask if that person could stay afterward and discuss it then.

Inviting Seekers

How do we invite people to come to a seeker discussion? We usually worry the most about this aspect, but it actually isn't as hard as some imagine.

Nancy's approach. Here's what Nancy did: "In the months leading up to the Bible study, I daily prayed that God would give me boldness and fill me with his Spirit. I also prayed daily for the women I planned to invite. I actually wrote out my 'invitation speech' on a note card. I was still feeling nervous, so I called my husband and asked him if I could practice on him! With his encouragement, I started inviting people— some by phone, others in person. My biggest surprise was how many at least agreed to come and check it out. I'd tell them, 'Try it for a few weeks. If it isn't your cup of tea, then don't worry about it.'

"I invited a new neighbor on my block who said, 'Sorry, I don't do Bible study.' By then my confidence had started to build so I answered, 'Well at least come to our first coffee, meet some of your neighbors and listen to what we're going to do!' She came, had a great time but still didn't come to the seeker study. That's okay—God has his time to reach her. Don't feel defeated if some people say they have a schedule conflict. Just tell them to come whenever they can and that if they want to come late, that's fine too."

Carol's approach. Carol, one of the coleaders in our study, has an amazing gift with people. She invited friends, casual acquaintances and total strangers to come to our seeker groups:

"Believe it or not, inviting people is the easy part, because it is God's work. He knows exactly who he wants to be at that seeker study. All we have to do is be willing to open our mouths and say the words 'Will you come?'

"When Nancy told me that she and Becky wanted to start a seeker Bible discussion in our neighborhood, I could barely contain my excitement. I took inventory of all my friends who didn't work on Tuesday afternoon and called them on the phone and said, 'Hey, guess what? My neighbor is starting up a Bible discussion, and it's for anyone who has always wanted to know what the Bible says but has never had time to find out. You don't have to know anything about the Bible. In fact, the more questions you have the better! Come with me on Tuesday and just see what you think, okay?' I'm sure some of my friends said 'okay' without really knowing why they were coming. Some may have said they'd come because they didn't want to disappoint me. I didn't care. I kept thinking, *Is this a great opportunity or what?*

"I also invited perfect strangers—it didn't matter. I remember calling Nancy one day and saying, 'I met two women while I was walking my dogs. I don't know their names or anything about them, but they said they were coming.' For that whole week before Tuesday, whenever we were taking inventory of who was coming, we referred to those women as 'the walkers.' Thank goodness we had name tags on Tuesday, and I finally learned their names! Amazingly, those two women have recently given their lives to Christ!

"One morning I ran into an acquaintance while I was out walking my dogs. As we spoke, she said she needed to get back so she could get a cup of coffee. I told her I was glad to be up so early because it would give me more time for my 'quiet time.' She asked me what a 'quiet time' was. I told her it was my time with God when I read my Bible and prayed.

"She looked wistfully at me and said, 'I wish I knew more about the Bible so I could have more quiet in my life.' Bingo! I invited her to the study and she said yes.

"Not everyone I've invited said yes. Some have said no, and that's okay. I never take 'no' as a 'never.' I keep loving them and praying for them and waiting for God's timing. One of these days, the time will be right and they'll come. So don't be discouraged if you ask thirty and only two show up—that means those are the two that the Lord wants there. Remember, it's his work, not ours. He just asks us to be faithful—to sow the seed. He'll take care of the harvest. The time is short and we have much to do. But isn't it exciting to be about our Father's business?"

Principles for Inviting People

- Before you invite anyone remember to pray in faith! "Nothing is impossible with God," Jesus says. Ask God to guide you to the people he wants you to ask, but be open to inviting everyone. As you cast the net wide, you may be very surprised who is interested in coming. Also be sure to enlist prayer support!

- Be enthusiastic! Assume a positive attitude, not a "you wouldn't want to come to this Bible discussion, would you?" attitude. Never assume that a person couldn't possibly be interested just because he or she seems far from the kingdom.

- Discover their point of need or interest and start from there.

- When possible, take time to build friendships with those you want to invite. However, don't exclude someone you don't know—just look at Carol's example!

- Assure them that knowledge of the Bible isn't necessary, nor do they have to accept that Jesus is God. This is for open-minded seekers who want to explore what the Bible says so they can make an intelligent decision.

- Decide on the time and place for the first meeting before you invite someone. Once you gather, you can decide the specifics there. (At the first meeting, for example, everyone may decide that it's more convenient to meet at a different time.) Ask them to come for this one meeting just to see if it is their cup of tea. Tell them they aren't signing up for a lifetime!

- Remind those you have invited of the place and time with a follow-up phone call the day before the study. Offer to pick them up if it's convenient.

- Write down what you want to say in your invitation. Practice with someone else first if you need to. You don't have to be having a serious spiritual conversation in order to invite someone. Just be enthusiastic and positive.

- At the first meeting you may say how long the study will be (usually six to eight weeks). But in the initial invitation I tend to say it will be for "several weeks."

Examples for Inviting Someone

For a neighborhood study or a study with coworkers. How do you approach a neighbor or a colleague whom you know only casually and with whom you haven't had a spiritual conversation in a while, or ever? You still open the conversation positively by assuming he or she would be interested: "Hey, you won't believe what some of our neighbors [or employees] are going to do! Because all of us are interested in spiritual topics and some of us don't know the Bible very well, we are going to meet at X's home [or at the conference room] for several weeks to study the Bible. You don't have to know what you believe or have read the Bible. This study is for anyone with an open mind who has honest questions and who wants to see what the Bible says so we can make up our own minds. I think it'll be fun. Think of it as a book club. We have our first meeting on Tuesday at 1:00. Can you join us? I'd love for you to come!"

For someone with whom you are already having a conversation about spiritual things. Perhaps this is a person whom you know fairly well and with whom you have had a few spiritual conversations. You might say, "I so enjoy talking to you about spiritual things. I'm about to start something I think you'd be interested in. I am having a seeker Bible discussion for people who aren't exactly sure what they believe but who are willing to discuss spiritual issues with each other. We will be reading the Gospel of John, one of the biographies of Jesus. We'll meet for several weeks for just an hour or so. Why don't you come once and see if you like it. I know you would add a lot to our discussions! The first meeting is at . . ."

For people raised in the church. What about people who consider themselves Christians because they have a church background but who don't seem to have a close walk with the Lord? Perhaps you are listening to them sort out a problem. You might say, "You know, as I hear you talking about your pain, I wonder if you'd find help in a seeker Bible discussion I am having. We will be meeting for several weeks to look at the Gospels and try to understand who Jesus really is. There's no pressure to believe. But it's for people who are trying to find real answers to life's problems. Life is tough, and we need all the help we can get. I know your grandma took you to Sunday school just like me. We were both raised in the church, but now we're adults and we need to understand how faith can help us make sense out of our lives right now. Why don't you come just for one time?"

TOUGH
QUESTIONS

I am frequently asked a number of questions when I talk to people about doing seeker Bible discussions.

"I'd like to do a seeker study, but how can I find the time?"

Maybe you feel your schedule is so crowded that you don't have the time to be involved in a seeker Bible discussion. The hostess of our Naperville discussion, Nancy, knew Julia was involved in many Christian activities, but she also knew Julia had a heart for seekers and that she'd be a great addition to our study. Here's Julia's story:

"When Nancy asked me to come to the seeker study and bring a seeker friend, I was already involved in so many Christian activities that I was hesitant. Besides my numerous church commitments, I had a leadership position in a Bible study with women from my church. Yet as I thought about it, I realized the majority of my time and ministry was spent with people within my own church walls. Still, when Nancy invited me to join this seeker study, I felt I could not commit to another Bible study. However, I make no decisions in my life without prayer. So I told God that if he brought me a seeker who had questions about faith, and who was willing to come, then I would come with her as well. A few days later I happened to see a former neighbor. We began chatting and catching up on our lives, and so I said, 'Would you be interested in coming to a Bible study for seekers to see if the Bible has anything relevant to say to our lives?' I was expecting a resounding 'NO!' so I wasn't very anxious about asking her. Instead, she enthusiastically agreed to come. Not only that, she did not flinch at the fifty-minute commute. Well, that was my answer. I knew God wanted me in that study.

"I watched in those first few months as women young and old eagerly soaked in life lessons from the Scriptures. I saw how positively they responded to this safe place—where they could admit, without shame, to having no knowledge of the Bible and to having unanswered questions, where they could learn and ask questions without feeling judged. The group grew so rapidly that by the second year we needed to break up into separate Bible studies. Again I prayed, and I felt called to lead one of the studies.

The whole experience has been so good for me. I have become sensitive to other people's backgrounds and traditions. I have learned so much from the questions seekers have and how they think. Besides the joy of seeing what is happening in the lives of these women, this has been such a significant spiritual journey for me, a journey that has led me to see the truth about Jesus Christ in exciting and new ways."

Even though Julia didn't think she could handle another activity, she still prayed about it. But she didn't stop at prayer—she was obedient and took a risk. These are often the missing ingredients when we ask for guidance. When we say, "Let me pray about it," it's usually our polite way of saying, "No way!" But Julia let God answer her prayer for guidance with his will, not hers. God answered unmistakably, Julia obeyed, and she has been a blessing to so many!

"I just feel too inadequate. What if I blow it and turn people off to God?"

A delightful woman named Stephne attended one of my Saltshaker conferences. Her story is a wonderful example of how God works through our inadequacies and fears:

"I'd never been trained to lead a seeker Bible discussion, and I'd also never seen a model I wanted to follow. What's worse, I'm a Christian and a pastor's wife, so I'm supposed to be good at this. When I went to Becky's Seeker Bible Study training conference, part of me was glad. I hoped I'd finally get an idea for what I should do. The rest of me felt the usual dread, failure and guilt. But by the end of the weekend, some of my deepest fears had been addressed. I learned how to invite seekers in a way that wasn't obnoxious. I learned that it wasn't up to me to make sure somebody got saved—only God can convert a soul. I learned that I could be a fellow learner and joyful participant in reading the Bible together with a seeker. My job was to be faithful, obedient and sensitive to the leading of the Holy Spirit. I didn't have to have all Bible knowledge either.

"I left feeling I had two very important tools in my possession: a Scripture-based, well-constructed seeker Bible study guide and a sensitive way of approaching people. Furthermore, by the end of the weekend I *knew* God wanted me to lead a seeker Bible discussion. I had the training, the tools, the guidance—and guess what? I still didn't want to, because I was scared I'd blow it.

"But all of my good reasons—shyness, a recent move, my task-orientated personality that didn't want to take the time to invest in people—didn't faze God a bit. He'd requested something of me, and there was only one good answer—complete obedience. I told God I would do it but he would have to bring someone to me, because I had all of these good 'reasons' not to do it. Then I prayed something even crazier. I told him that though I was serious about leading a seeker discussion, this first time he would have to send a seeker who'd ask *me* to do a Bible discussion. Now what's the likelihood of that happening? But my prayer was serious and from the heart.

"Would you believe that a short time later a woman, who had only recently started visiting our church, walked up to me and said in a no-nonsense tone, 'I want to have a Bible study, and I'd like you to lead it.' After my initial shock, I asked her why. She said, 'God doesn't answer my prayers. Maybe if I get to know him better he'll answer me.'

"At that time I was in the middle of moving, so I promised we'd set a date when the move was over. Secretly I was hoping she'd just forget about it. But oh no. After my move I called her, and she said she was ready. God, faithful as usual, helped me to let go of my 'reasons' and fears and told me to use my newly learned tools to minister to this woman. I went and led my first seeker discussion.

"It's been such an exciting experience. On the outside everything about this woman looks perfect: she has a very successful job and great looks—yet she's been through real pain, and as it turns out, she has lots of inner doubts. When we started the study, she was businesslike and very task-oriented. But each week she seemed to soften. She couldn't get over how Jesus treated the woman at the well and how he showed her respect and love when everyone around her rejected her. We have only one more study to go in John, but she just told me she wants to start up again after Christmas. But this time I told the Lord he can send me more people if he wants. In fact, I just may invite them myself!"

Isn't it wonderful how God answers our prayers! Stephne was faithful, and look at the confidence she gained after just one study.

"But I'm a pastor. Wouldn't seekers feel awkward in my presence?"

Pastor Marty, a minister of a large, affluent church, recently attended one of my Saltshaker conferences, bringing a group from his church. I discovered he not only has a great passion for evangelism but is very familiar with seeker Bible discussions:

"Early in my pastoral ministry, I stumbled on the idea of starting a seeker Bible discussion. We were living in North Hollywood, California, at the time, and God gave my wife and me a heart for several unbelieving neighbors. In an effort to introduce them to Christ, I invited them to join a small Bible study we were holding in another neighbor's house.

"My wife and I love to entertain in our own home, but from the outset it seemed to us that seekers (especially our neighbors) were often reticent to come to a 'pastor's home' for a Bible study. Over the years we have usually led such groups in the home of a neighbor with whom other seeking neighbors will be more at ease. This also takes my wife and me out of our comfortable surroundings where we 'know how to act,' forcing us to relate to seekers on their turf. The result is that our leadership becomes more sensitive and less threatening.

"I came to Becky's evangelism training conference because through her books and speaking I had come to respect her ability to ask the right questions that truly connect with unchurched individuals. I was eager to see, and hopefully use, her seeker studies. As I had anticipated, I came away having learned new ways to pose probing yet safe questions when leading seekers in the study of God's Word.

"I determined at that conference that beginning in January I would begin a seeker Bible discussion for neighbors using Becky's John studies. But I faced my same old dilemma: would my neighbors feel uncomfortable coming to our home since I am a pastor? While I was at the conference, a thought came to me. Normally we think of the 'host family' of a seeker discussion being a fellow Christian. But what if I asked the most unlikely non-Christian on our block to host it? And I knew immediately who that would be! A couple that my wife and I once christened 'the model and the muscleman.' When they first moved into the neighborhood three years ago, we jokingly said to one another, 'Now *there's* a likely couple to host our next Bible study!' Yet as Becky spoke I couldn't shake the idea. After traveling home, I e-mailed Becky and asked her what she thought of the idea. She said it was 'inspired!' As of this writing we have invited that couple, and they have enthusiastically agreed to join our January study. They are even open (though they haven't given a definite 'yes') to hosting it in their home.

"Why do I feel strongly about doing a seeker discussion as a pastor? The reason I involve myself in seeker Bible discussions is twofold. First, I have come to believe that I am as accountable to God for how I conduct myself and communicate his love to my neighbors as I am for how I preach to the members of my congregation. Second, I have found nothing else that keeps me so in touch with the language, priorities, thought processes, longings and hurts of the very people I want my congregation to reach for Christ. I am convinced that my continuing effectiveness and fruitfulness in ministry is tied directly to the time I spend with these precious seekers. I owe so much to them for all they have taught me (and continue to teach me) about my own humanity and about Christ's love for us all and the transforming power of God's Word."

How I wish every pastor in America could read and emulate what Pastor Marty is doing!

"But don't seeker discussions work best for white suburban women?"

I recently led a one-day training conference on seeker Bible study in Chicago. By God's grace there are now seeker studies using *Looking at the Life of Jesus* in many parts of the Chicago area. There are studies for women and couples in the suburbs, and for young professionals in the city. There are office studies for coworkers, studies at a halfway house for men recently released from prison or in rehab for drugs, and a study for Hispanic families. African Americans, Caucasians and Hispanics; the wealthy and the poor; the well-educated and the uneducated; executives and convicts; people from the suburbs and from the inner city—all are reading God's Word and encountering Jesus!

So much in life separates us—age, race, gender—but the Bible is the one thing that can reach everyone, regardless of our nationality, race or socioeconomic background. Reverend Wayne Gordon, a pastor of a thriving African American church in the heart of inner-city Chicago, has this to say about the effectiveness of seeker Bible discussions for reaching all types of people:

"Being the pastor of an African American church on Chicago's west side, I have used seeker Bible discussions for over twenty-five years. In fact, our church was birthed when my wife, Anne, and I led seeker discussions for high school kids. Today I lead a seeker discussion with fifty men who have just gotten out of prison or have come into our Hope House straight off the streets. Most are addicted to drugs yet want to get some help. It is through our seeker Bible discussion that God begins the transformation of their lives.

"Our seeker group teaches the Bible from a very basic and nonreligious point of view. The men are eager to learn ways to put their lives back together. We find that over seventy-five percent of the men commit their lives to Christ as a result of our discussions. I know of no better way to teach unchurched people about the love of Christ than through the study of God's Word in a sensitive and nonjudgmental manner as in a seeker discussion."

"What about child-care?"

Two women who attended one of my evangelism training conferences wanted to start a seeker Bible discussion for young moms in their neighborhood. The problem was child-care. The moms couldn't afford to hire baby sitters on a weekly basis, and the leaders didn't have the room to handle both groups. Not to be detoured, these enterprising women asked their pastor if they could use one of the church rooms for their seeker discussions on the same day the church offered other classes that provided child-care. The pastor was thrilled with their vision for evangelism and said yes. Without realizing it, they accomplished two significant things: the moms were able to study the Bible, and the children were not only cared for but began to develop relationships with children from Christian families.

While I would usually encourage seeker discussions to meet someplace more neutral than a church, this situation worked out beautifully. Another woman who attended my seeker-Bible-discussion training found a godly older woman from her church to babysit the children while their mothers attended the seeker discussions.

"Are there any differences in doing a couples' seeker study?"

The principles of any seeker study are pretty much the same. A couples' study is ideal for neighborhoods, especially if you have established a few friendships as couples. A married couple may share the leadership or choose one to lead and the other to colead. Feel free to invite a few Christians to attend so long as the majority of participants are not believers.

BRINGING
PEOPLE TO CHRIST

While our ultimate desire is for people to commit their lives to Christ, our immediate goal is for each person to respond positively to the real Jesus revealed in the Scriptures. It's easy to get discouraged if we don't see people commit their lives to Christ right away, but we need to be patient. God's timetable is the one that counts—not our own. Success for one person may be coming to a seeker discussion as a hostile skeptic but leaving impressed for the first time by the person of Jesus and the love and authenticity of Christians. Conversion is a process, and whether God uses us to help someone cross the threshold between belief and unbelief or to simply help the seeker take the next step toward conversion—all of it is valuable in the kingdom of God. We need to remember that we don't decide who becomes a Christian. When a person comes to Christ, it is the result of God's enormous grace and the receptivity of the seeker's soul; we cannot *make* it happen. Redemption is God's business from start to finish—we are there to point the way to Christ.

Once, toward the end of a sixteen-week seeker discussion, we were reading John's account of the crucifixion. I asked, "Why do you think Jesus insisted on dying?" One woman said, "Well, don't you think the real problem in human nature is simply ignorance? We just need more education." I was so disappointed. Here I felt I had adequately explained the problem of sin several times before, and she still didn't get it. I responded by saying, "While it is true that we need to be informed about God, I don't think the Bible suggests that the heart of the problem is a result of being uneducated. Look at Nazi Germany—here was a culture that gave us brilliant literature, music and philosophers, and yet they were responsible for one of the greatest atrocities ever to occur on our planet. No, the problem is deeper than a lack of knowledge—it's the problem of sin."

I went home feeling very down, and I wondered, *What's the use? Will they ever get it?* But the very next week the same woman came up to me absolutely glowing and said, "Becky, you won't believe this. My aging father is an atheist, and he just told me he is afraid of dying and wanted to know if I knew anything about the Bible. I told him I was reading it for the first time in my life, and I asked him if he would like to read the Gospel of John with me. So we are starting next week! Since I've been coming to this study I started praying for him. I think this is a miracle!"

I immediately felt convicted. I realized in that moment that I was seeing success from God's point of view. True, she didn't fully understand the gospel yet, but she was moving in the right direction. I needed to be patient, give up my timetable and let her grow at her own pace.

Explaining the Gospel

Just because we are studying Scriptures doesn't mean we are necessarily presenting the gospel in a formal sense. The truth is, there are many ways to understand and explain the gospel. (I would suggest you read chapter twelve in *Out of the Saltshaker* and the appendix for further reading to help you understand the gospel.) Jesus never explained the gospel in the same way twice. Certainly being exposed to Jesus is a great place to begin. But just because someone studies Jesus for eight weeks doesn't necessarily mean they will understand the Creator Father or the problem of sin or how we are to respond and make faith our own. So what should we do?

First, let them see who Jesus is. Sometimes we will be able to draw other aspects of the gospel message—including the problem of sin—from the passage we are reading. Another way to share the essence of the gospel is through individual contacts outside the Bible discussions. I have often met with a person for lunch, praying God would give me the opportunity to explain the essence of the gospel. Other times, but not always, toward the end of the study I have said, "We have been reading about Jesus, but some of you may wonder, *Just what does it mean to become a Christian or to be one?* So let me take five minutes to explain it." One needs to be sensitive to the prompting of the Spirit.

The first year I led the Naperville discussion group, for example, I asked the Lord how I was to end the last week of our study. I didn't feel led to present the gospel formally, so I asked the Lord to use some creative way to make the gospel clear. Just as I finished the passage on John 20, Mary, "the intellectual" that Diann wrote about earlier, said, "Becky, if I understand what I've been reading for the last seven weeks, am I right to assume that the Bible says the central crisis of the human condition is the problem of sin?"

"Yes," I answered.

"Okay, will you go over one more time what the nature of sin is?"

"It's having a God-complex. It's our determination, through our pride and unbelief, to run our own lives rather than let God be in charge. Sin is choosing to be self-ruled rather than God-ruled. And sin has left us addicted to ourselves," I answered.

"So the solution to the problem of sin is the death of Christ, right?" she asked.

"Right," I answered.

"Okay, go over one more time how Christ's death solves the problem of sin."

I gulped and asked the Lord to help me. "God sent his Son, Jesus, to pay for the mess we've created. We deserved God's judgment, but Jesus stepped in and took it for us. He sacrificed his life for us and overcame our sin so we could have a fresh start. He also rose from the dead and offers to forgive our sins and make us whole," I answered.

"Last question," Mary asked, "How do you make this your own?"

I told the group a story of a person who had recently committed his life to Christ. Then I said, "All we need to do is surrender our lives to him, to repent and believe." Mary dissolved in tears, and God used her to close our discussion that year in an incredibly powerful way. Yet it was another year before Mary gave her life to Christ.

One way to share the gospel is to give each person in your seeker discussion *The Way of Jesus*. This is a resource I wrote specifically for seekers to help them understand the cross. I suggest that you give it to your seeker friends and meet with them individually to talk about what they understand. If you're leading a seeker study, you may want to give each participant a copy of *The Way of Jesus* as your study is about to terminate. Suggest that you meet one more time to discuss the content of the book.

When Someone Becomes a Christian

People come to Christ in so many different ways through a seeker discussion. But once they have given their lives to Christ, we should meet with them individually for several weeks. We need to talk with them about the importance of church and help them find a worshiping community where they fit. The issue of church attendance is vital once they have become a Christian. The seeker study is not a substitute for church. They may, as a young believer, want to continue in the seeker study. But they also need to become active in a local church. Then we need to gently teach them about the spiritual disciplines: personal devotions, prayer and so on.

Mary is a great example. Carol began meeting with Mary after she gave her life to Christ. One day after prayer, Carol invited Mary to her own church. Finding the right church for someone with such a good mind was a bit daunting, but Carol felt sure she would respond to her pastor. The results have been thrilling. Mary came and was deeply moved by the sermon and awed by the worship. In fact, she got the sermon tape and began circulating it among all her friends. Two weeks later Mary and her husband went to the church together. Our prayer is that they will join soon.

Discerning If Someone Has Become a Christian

Periodically throughout the seeker discussions I say, "There will probably come a time when one of you feels God is nudging you to do something. Maybe it's to obey something you read in the Bible this week, maybe it's mending a relationship, or maybe you realize that you have never really let Christ be the center of your life. When that time comes, would you let me [or one of the leaders] know?" Often, regardless of the area of conviction, we find that if they are ready to meet with us individually, they are usually ready to receive Christ.

Other times I say, "Maybe you've wondered, *How much do I have to know in order to give my life unconditionally to*

Christ? I would say one good place to start is here: Give as much as you understand about yourself to as much as you understand about Jesus. And if you want to make this commitment, please be sure to tell someone!"

Usually it's over a lunch or a private meeting that I get a better sense of where someone is spiritually. And don't be afraid to ask direct questions when you talk with someone after the seeker discussion. I once asked Mary, after trust had developed and I felt she was probably ready to become a Christian, "How have you changed as a result of being in this study? Where do you feel you are now on your spiritual journey?"

She answered, "That's a very important question, and I want to think about it before I answer."

Three weeks later she approached me after the Bible study and told me she had asked Christ to be the Lord of her life. While in that second year of our study she had intellectually already accepted that Christianity was true, it was my question that pushed her to make a personal decision.

WHAT ARE MY
NEXT STEPS?

If you are considering starting a seeker Bible discussion, begin with prayer. Ask the Lord to give you increased faith and boldness to be a witness for Jesus. Jesus said, "I tell you the truth, if you have faith as small as a mustard seed, you can say to this mountain, 'Move from here to there' and it will move. Nothing will be impossible for you" (Matthew 17:20). Ask the Lord to allow the message of Jesus to be communicated through you (Colossians 4:3). Pray every day, and expect God to set up divine appointments for you. Believe Jesus when he said the harvest is great and the laborers are few. Determine that you will obey him, and expect God to do great things. Jesus encouraged us to pray boldly: "I tell you the truth, my Father will give you whatever you ask in my name. Until now you have not asked for anything in my name. Ask and you will receive, and your joy will be complete" (John 16:23-24).

Focus on Your Friends

Make a list of all the non-Christians you know personally. Look at the people with whom your life naturally intersects. Think through your relationships in your family, at work or school, in your neighborhood or dormitory, at the gym or tennis club, among your friends. Pray over your list regularly, asking God for direction, favor and wisdom. Go through your list slowly before God. Ask God to draw them toward himself and to open their eyes to the emptiness of life without him. Ask God to make them aware of their need and to remove their defenses toward faith. As you go about your day, ask God, "Is *she* the person you want to reach through me? Is *he*?" It's an exciting way to live.

Build genuine friendships with the people you are called to be a witness to. God wants us to communicate care and love to the people he has brought into our lives. Caring involves listening, getting involved with their concerns, being available even when it's not convenient. We do not have to be someone's best friend in order to share Christ, but inviting someone for dinner can go a long way.

Seek Guidance

Spend time in prayer, asking the Lord for clear guidance. Ask God what your role should be. Maybe God isn't calling you to lead a seeker discussion but to host a group or be a coleader. Maybe he is calling you to be an active participant in a seeker discussion that is already formed, which involves committing yourself to attending regularly and to bringing at least one seeker friend. God knows what he wants you to do, so ask him. Share your fears, and ask him to give you courage.

Consider Partnership

Ask God if there is another believer you can work with. Pray about whether God has a coleader who will share your vision, pray with you, invite seekers and support you. It's usually helpful to have a second Christian in the group, especially in a group of more than five people. Ecclesiastes 4:9-12 says, "Two are better than one, because they have a good return for their work: If one falls down, his friend can help him up! . . . Though one may be overpowered, two can defend themselves. A cord of three strands is not quickly broken." If you can't find a coleader, then go ahead and trust that God will work through you.

Think Through Some Basic Questions

Who? Decide who you are going to invite, and ask God to open their hearts to be willing to come. Initiate a social opportunity, such as a meal or a social event, and ask God to provide an opening to invite them to the discussion. Even inviting by telephone is acceptable so long as you are comfortable with it.

What? Determine what kind of group you feel called to: neighbors, coworkers, tennis partners, teens. Is it a small group (one or two people), medium-sized group (three to five) or a larger group (six to twelve)? The size of the group will influence decisions such as where you will meet and whether you need a host and a coleader. You may be more comfortable at first beginning with only one seeker, which can be a very powerful and meaningful experience. But the group could be four, eight, or as many as fourteen or twenty. Some feel the ideal size for a group is three to eight, but I have found just about any size works so long as the leader feels comfortable. But whatever the configuration, *not more than half the members should be believers.* Preferably there should be only two believers for every six non-Christians. This insures that it doesn't turn into a "Christian" discussion where seekers feel ill at ease and Christians answer all the questions and dominate the discussion.

Also decide what you want to study. Usually it's best to begin with a Gospel, and I prefer starting with John or Luke.

Where? Both the type of people and the size of the group will determine the place. For example, when Kathy, a top professional at a consumer products company, decided to start a seeker discussion for coworkers, she realized immediately that the most convenient place and time for everyone was the conference room during the lunch hour. If you are leading a one-on-one study, it will most likely be held at your place or theirs. If you want to have a large study, then find someone willing to host it.

When? When the seeker discussion should take place depends on who is coming. For example, if it's a neighborhood study for women who do not work, daytime is usually better; if it's a study for couples or for working people, then evening is better.

How? There are essentially two ways to start. Either you can have a kick-off meeting, like we did with the coffee gathering, or you can start the study the first time you meet. The value of a kick-off is that the group can meet each other, decide on the time that suits the most people and ask any questions they may have. Just pick the approach that works best for you.

What If They Want to Continue?

What if your seeker group wants to continue meeting, as has happened in our Naperville study? I am currently preparing other seeker Bible discussions. You can check my website (www.saltshaker.org) for availability. You can also select a good Bible study guide for Christians and adapt the questions and applications to seekers. After leading a seeker study for only eight weeks, you will develop a sense of what works and what doesn't in your study.

Why Do Seeker Discussions?

Why do we do seeker discussions? Because God uses them to bring people to himself. Of all the stories of changed lives that have emerged from our Naperville seeker discussion, there is one that moves me to tears. Every week when Mary walked to our Tuesday study, she would invariably encounter a couple who lived on the corner of her block. Since they saw her carrying a Bible, they assumed she was religious. They declared outright that they were agnostics. She found it amusing that they teased her relentlessly with comments like, "Oh there goes the Bible lady today" or "Here comes da Saint!" She always laughed and responded with a quip, but thought to herself, *If you only knew me better!*

But soon after she became a Christian she was astonished to receive a phone call from the wife saying, "Mary, you know my husband and I are not religious. But he has just been diagnosed with cancer, and the doctors tell us he doesn't have much time left. He's in the hospital, and he wants a little more time to say his goodbyes. Would you ask that Bible group of yours to pray that Ron will be given more time?"

Mary walked in the door that Tuesday stunned by their request. It was the first time anyone had ever asked her to pray for them, and she was astounded by who had made the request! We assured Mary that we would pray.

Two weeks later Mary had this to report: "Sue called me this morning to say that Ron was just released from the hospital. The doctors were astonished by how he suddenly turned around. They now think he has several months left. Sue wanted me to thank you from the bottom of her heart."

Mary remained in contact with Sue, and a friendship developed. Mary also introduced Ron and Sue to Carol, one of the coleaders of the study. But two months later, Ron went into a rapid decline. One day Sue called Mary and asked her to come over right away. Ron was dying. Being a new believer, Mary felt she needed spiritual backup, so she called Carol and asked her to come to their home too. As Mary entered the front door she saw Ron lying on a bed in the living room with many family members gathered around him. She was so grateful when Carol walked in the door that she confidently announced, as only a new believer could, "Carol is here. Now let us hold hands and Carol will pray." Carol tried not to show her nervousness at praying so unexpectedly before total strangers. But after she finished her prayer she knew she had to do more.

Carol asked Sue for permission to speak directly to her husband Ron. Ron, on morphine, looked so out of it and seemed to be in a coma, but Carol knew this was her only chance. So in front of the entire family she looked into Ron's face, took his lifeless hand in hers, and said in a loud voice, "Ron! This is Carol. You need to listen to me because I have something very important to say to you." Later Sue told Carol that she knew he was hearing everything she said because the minute she called out his name his eyebrows shot straight up.

"Ron, do you remember when the twin towers collapsed and we saw those firemen racing up the stairs to rescue as many people as possible, with no thought for themselves? Do you remember how awed we were by their bravery and courage—how they were willing to risk their lives to save the lives of others? Ron, that is nothing compared to what Christ has done for you! He came to earth two thousand years ago to rescue all of us. We needed to be rescued from all our mistakes, all the wrong things we have done in our lives. None of us is perfect, Ron, and when the time comes to stand before our Maker who *is* perfect, we would all stand rightfully condemned. But Christ came to sacrifice himself for us; he took our place. All you need to do is say 'yes' to what Jesus did on the cross. You are going to be entering eternity soon, and I want to know you are going to the home Jesus has prepared for you. You can go to your *true home,* Ron. All you need to do is say 'yes' to Jesus."

Later Carol told me, "I couldn't tell if he understood what I was saying. After I left I wondered, *How could I have said it better?* I felt really discouraged that night as I prayed for him.

"The next morning Sue called and told me Ron had died about a half an hour earlier, and she asked me if I would come over. I drove over thinking I would find Sue in a terrible state. But when she opened the door, she had this incredible smile on her face. Then she said to me, 'You will never believe what happened thirty minutes ago. Ron had not spoken a word in days, and whatever he attempted to say was incoherent. Then suddenly he opened his eyes and looked at me with a peace and a joy I have never seen in him—ever. He smiled at me and said, "Going home now."

'I said, "Ron, you are home."

'And he said, "No, my true home. The real home." He looked at me with a radiance I could scarcely believe and he died.'

As Carol told me later, "Becky, there is no doubt in my mind that Ron not only heard me, but he said 'yes' to Jesus. I had prayed that if Ron had accepted Christ, God would let someone know. And God did. Can you imagine the impact this had on Mary as a young believer? I told Mary, 'You are one of the reasons that Ron is in heaven today. You responded to their initial request for prayer, you were a faithful friend through their crisis, and you called me in when you felt you needed some backup!' "

Why do I continue to do seeker discussions year after year? It's simple. I am in awe over how Jesus Christ changes lives. Won't you participate in the adventure too?

For more information on Rebecca Pippert's training conferences through Saltshaker Ministries, or for helpful hints on leading seeker studies, visit her website at
<<www.saltshaker.org>>